Advance Praise for
Reflections of Us

"Poets must learn how to balance looking out the window while staring at the mirror. Zenobia Lundy in her first collection of poems writes about the community that surrounds her while looking at her own reflection. Poets are either observers or witnesses, the difference being the degree of compassion they show and feel for their fellow human beings. Lundy's poems are wrapped in simplicity and tenderness. Outside the window she sees the hopelessness and the hope. *Reflections of Us* teaches us how to survive; these poems could be elders in a church, humming with the choir while fanning their fans. At the center of Lundy's book is the goodness we all need in order to celebrate another day."

— E. Ethelbert Miller, writer and literary activist,
author of *When Your Wife Has Tommy John Surgery
and Other Baseball Stories*

"In *Reflections of Us*, Zenobia's verses offer inspiration and insight into her life as a reflection of the times. They respond to family, love, marriage, children, neighbors, events, and to her need to write. Although interwoven with the social justice struggles of the past sixty years, her observations 'gently ... rest / in the womb of her past.'"

— J. C. Todd, author of *Beyond Repair*

Reflections of Us

A POETRY COLLECTION

ZENOBIA

Copyright ©2021 by Zenobia Lundy

All rights reserved under International and Pan-American Copyright Conventions. Published in the United States by Tree of Life Books.

Publisher's Cataloging-In-Publication Data
Lundy, Zenobia
Refelctions of Us

ISBN: 978-1-7349563-4-4

Printed in the United States of America

First Edition

Editor/Publisher: Joy E. Stocke
Copyeditor: Raquel B. Pidal
Design and Composition: Tim Ogline / Ogline Design

Published by Tree of Life Books
PO Box 81
557 Rosemont-Ringoes Rd
Sergeantsville, New Jersey 08557

www.treeoflifetreeofjoy.com

Reflections of Us
A POETRY COLLECTION

ZENOBIA

Tree of Life Books

*What lies behind us
and what lies before us
are tiny matters
compared to what lies within us.*

– Henry Stanley Haskins

*The act of making art exposes a society to itself.
Art brings things to light. It illuminates us.
It sheds light on our lingering darkness.*

– Julia Cameron, author of *The Artist's Way*

Table of Contents

Introduction	X
Reflections of Us	1
Outside the Lines	2
My Street	3
Got Tired	4
Grits and Gravy	7
She	9
Who I Am	10
He	11
The Artist You Are	12
Close	13
Between the Lines	14
The Man on the Train	15
To Nora and Langston	17
Passing Through	18
Things	19
Colors	20
Forgotten	21
In and Out	22
The Place	23
Hey Lady	24
Too Much	26
Morning Coffee	27
I Write Because I Must	28
Grab a Star	29
Free Cups and Sullen Looks	30
A Piece of Metal	31
Old Woman	32

Hours for Dollars	33
Miss Annie	34
I Saw Colors	35
Poem for Mr. Bell	36
Again	37
Passing Through	38
Another Black Man	39
Memorial Day	41
The Ones	42
Sister of Honey, Caramel, and Ebony	43
I Saw Her	46
Half	47
Enough	48
The Queen	49
She II	50
Breonna	51
Scarlet Weaver	52
I Am	53
See Me	55
Greyhound Bus to Jersey, 1977	56
The Look	57
Lives	59
The Late	60
Walls	61
Words Will Make Us Think	62
Acknowledgements	63
About the Author	65

Introduction

I was born the year Emmett Till was murdered in Money, Mississippi, and raised in West Philadelphia, a daughter of the Great Migration of my Black brothers and sisters from the rural South (1916–1970) to Northern cities like Chicago, Philadelphia, and New York. As a child, I realized there were two Americas, the America of my middle-class Black neighborhood in West Philadelphia, and the other America.

I remember sitting in my elementary classroom the day President John F. Kennedy was assassinated. I can still see tears running down my teacher's face. President Kennedy had been our people's hope, the light at the end of a long, dark night. Even as a child I felt that light go out.

I also grew up in the turbulent birth of the civil rights movement with the battle for equality and justice that continues to this very day. The players have changed, but the struggle remains. I learned quickly that my America included people like James Brown and Angela Davis, reminding me to be Black and Proud, and that there were many people in the other America who hated me for one reason only: I am Black. The other America portrayed on the television screen was not the America I lived in.

Around this time, I began my love of reading and writing. Writing for me has become a way to express the love, the hurt, and all the feelings in between. Often, words were all I had to save me.

My writing has evolved as I have evolved. My early poems reflect love and loss. Like all young women, finding true love was a major part of my existence. My writings continue to reflect the journey of my life and the struggles in America to realize that we all matter.

Every time someone is mistreated, abused, imprisoned unjustly, killed, each of us is mistreated, abused, imprisoned unjustly, killed. As Martin Luther King said so eloquently, "Injustice anywhere is a threat to justice everywhere." Each of us reflects the world we live in. We create this world every day with our actions or inactions.

I also write about the beautiful parts of growing up Black in America. I love our music, our style, our heritage, and the way we do us. I genuinely believe that one person can make a difference in the world. And that world starts the minute our feet hit the floor every day. American writer and fellow poet Audre Lorde says it nicely: "It is not our differences that divide us. It is our inability to recognize and celebrate those differences."

Through my poems, I have tried to celebrate those differences. As we journey through life, we must learn to meet each person where they are regardless of race, age, economic status, disability, or any other difference they may have. We must learn to celebrate each life and each journey. For in this celebration, we truly learn to experience and enjoy life for all she is.

I believe that one person can make a difference. If everyone who reads or listens to my poems wakes up tomorrow and vows to make just one more person in the world happy, I will have completed the journey of this book. May those who read my poetry, or join me for a reading, see a reflection of us.

– Zenobia
West Philadelphia, 2021

*Until the lions have their own historians,
the history of the hunt will always glorify the hunter.*

– African Proverb

Reflections of Us

I see us in every
raindrop

Reflections of the

Hope of our mothers and fathers

Every note from every
saxophone that has ever been played

I see us
in every tear
from every mother who
has lost a son

Reflections of us
ripple through time and space
ropes burning our necks
cramped spaces below deck

Police dogs and billy clubs
and prison cells

They run through my mind again and again

Reflections of us
Our greatness, Our despair

Our love
Our depth

Outside the Lines

This world of mine
has no form
It runs outside the lines
I see its reflection in the faces
I meet
I see the homeless
I see the brokenhearted
I see babies dying on a distant shore
I see their mothers
I feel their pain

My heart hears the sorrows
of those behind prison bars
My soul yearns
to touch their pain
to ease their hurt

Come with me
Let's go outside the lines

My Street

There are no flowers
    on my street
No hope

Fear greets me
    with each new day
on my street

We can't be friends   on my street
And you must look hard to
   find the sun   on my street

Even the birds fly high   on my street
No one comes to visit

Time goes slow   on my street

And if you're not careful
You can fall between the cracks

      on my street

Got Tired

It was hard for us
He was White
and I was Black
And many times, we
had to jump off buses
And leave early
and come late

Endure the stares

But I knew he loved me …

You ask
What happened?

I think I just got tired
of
Jumping off buses
Leaving early
Coming late
Enduring the Stares

But I loved him
in my way … and
he brought me coffee
from Famous Diner
on South Street
when it was just hippies
and old Black men

I hope he knew in his heart
that I loved him
Between the stares
Between time and space
I loved him
I just got tired

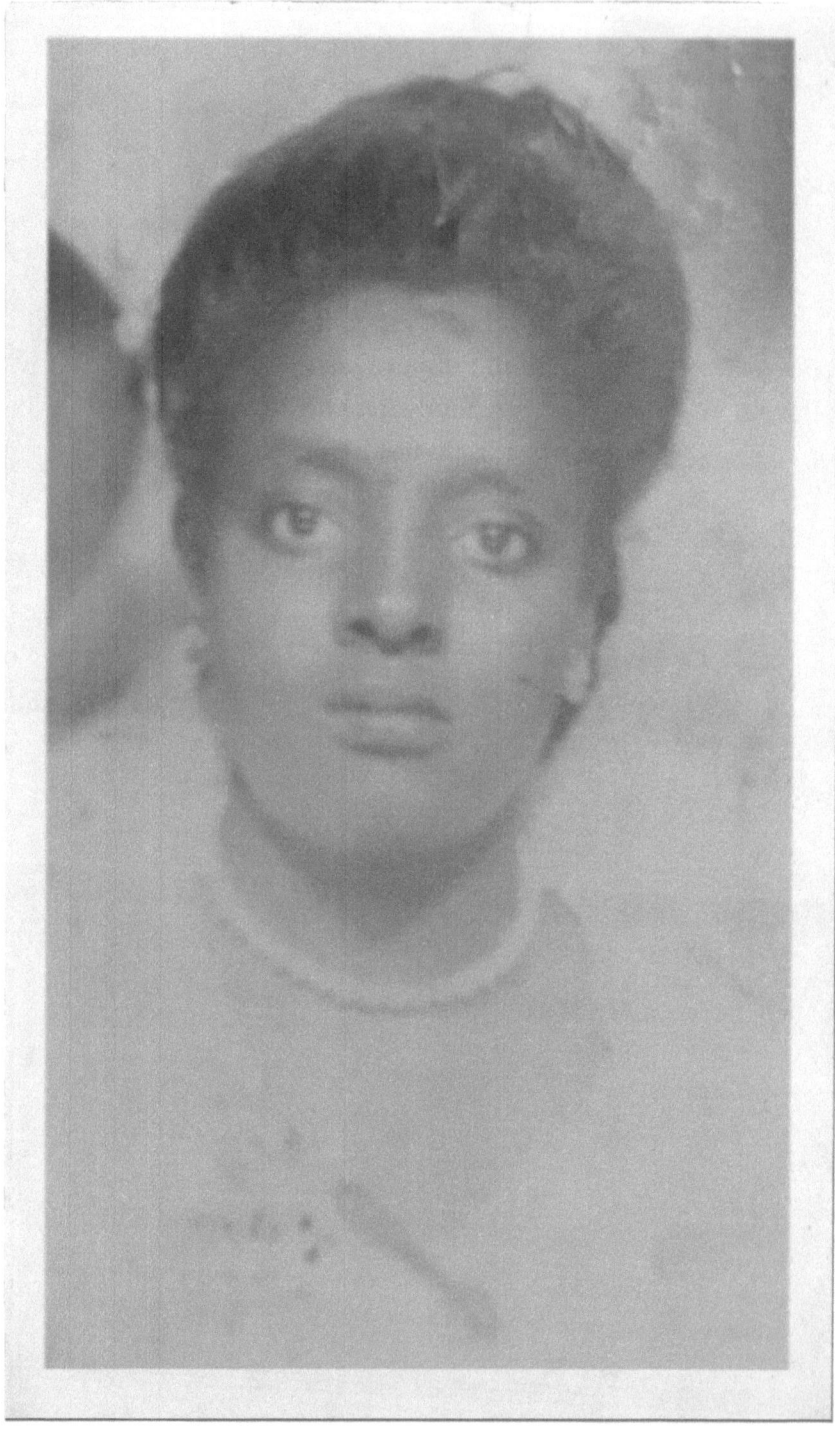

Grits and Gravy

She rose early every day
She made the best grits and gravy
She washed my clothes
sometimes in the tub
I remember her most in the kitchen
But sometimes in poodle skirts
all dressed up
Her hair cut short
Shiny lips
She had a spirit like sunshine
She was always on her way somewhere
Down South, church, work, bed
She never really settled down
in between the comings and goings
She loved me so
She carried me through
She loved me
She did her best

Only when our eyes can no longer see
and our arms can no longer touch
I realize
I should have held her close and squeezed her tight
She left suddenly like darkness at dawn
No goodbyes, no farewells
I miss her so
Her smiles
Her grits and gravy
The way she loved me
Her Sunday calls
Her voice so sweet
and her serious looks that etched my soul
Looks only a mother can give

She

She came softly by with hair of silver
and smiled at me

As we rummaged through clothes at the Goodwill
she asked me questions about this shirt
and that dress

I guess she thought I had style
And the skirt I picked she said it was sharp
And somehow when
I gave her my number
I knew
like leaves rising up on a crisp fall day
when she stood
with her profile against the setting sun
I knew
we would never meet again
and I knew
every time I wore that skirt
I would think of her

Who I Am

You ask me
who I am?
I am a poet
I have no patience
for endless
rambling words
sentences
paragraphs
or chapters
with beginnings
and no endings
I am a poet
Life comes to me in
fragments of joy
moments of pain
seconds of pleasure

He

He sits on the porch
Some call him crazy
He's always looking for a cigarette
and he's happy if he's got a pack

He remembers Mother's Day and Easter
He asked me if I'm going to church today
But sometimes he's busy talking to someone
I can't see

And you know it's cold if he's not there

It's kind of funny though
He's busy talking to someone else
But he always asks how I am

The Artist You Are

Your eyes see the world in a different way

Your hands create
what your heart feels

You will always be someone who

sees raindrops in silver
sunshine in yellow

And babies sound flamingo pink
And jazz makes you think…blue…

You are quiet
painting in your head

You open a window
so we can see

Close

so close there is no space
so close there are no stops
no periods no ends
blending melting
two become one

me you us
where do I begin and where do you end

mine yours ours

my top your bottom
the ins the outs

always us

we me one

Between the Lines

Too much energy
Too much talk
Too much time
Too much trying
Too many tears
To read between the lines

The Man on the Train

He sits in the
same seat every day
He waits for her
Like he's waiting for a lover
And even from behind
I can see the
twinkle in his eye
The apples of his cheeks
fill up
when she arrives
She sits down
a caress, shoulder to shoulder
just like lovers

For those
few minutes every day
he is happy

She gets off
She never looks back
The smile
leaves his face
and he becomes just another man on the train

To Nora and Langston

Your words echo in my mind
If I could have pulled around with you in Harlem
that would have been cool
You could have showed me the Savoy
and we could have went to see Du Bois
and I would've looked cool in a fur-trimmed coat
and a hat with a feather in it

Passing Through

When I am gone
find a picture of me smiling
Laughing when I was young
Huggin' my kids
Lovin' my man
Watering my flowers
Walking my dog
Sitting in the sun
Laying on the beach
That's where you will find me

An old dead woman in a box
that ain't me

Don't shed no tears
for that old woman

I was only passing through
I'm somewhere else now
Sitting on the beach
Watering my flowers
Walking my dog
Huggin' my kids
Lovin' my man

Things

Life hands you things

Things you do not understand
and things you can't fix
Things that hurt
Things that make you cry
and things that shake your very soul
When one thing leaves
another takes its place
You hold onto this life with faith and love
Somehow
you learn to deal with everything
Good things and bad things
And when you can't change a thing
write about it

Colors

Colors of the sky
Slow days and fast people
A look
A dying man
And when did a broken life become entertainment
A forgotten hello
A rolled eye
A stare
Are we not here together?
In this time
This space
If the bomb comes today
Won't we both die?

Forgotten

I see you in my dreams

I hear your voice in the night's stillness

Some say you have lost your voice
But you cry out to me
Bars separate you from your babies the ones you love

I have never met you
Not touched your hand or felt the wetness of your tears
or felt your fears

But oh, my sister you are my sister

Hair blowing in the wind
Now afraid lost
with no sun to warm your skin
I have not forgotten

In and Out

Caressing, flowing

Velvet, lace
so sweet to taste

Wet like rain
Violets, pinks

The wind blows
against the day

So gently she rests
in the womb of her past

The Place

Let me show you the place
the corner

The sun still shines there
That space in time remains

Children walk by
Birds fly above

A thousand days have
come and gone

Sunsets and sunrise
It never changes
the place where a son dies

Hey Lady

Hey lady gimme a quarter
My life is broken
I ain't eat today

Well only a bowl of oatmeal

Hey lady gimme a quarter

Too Much

With the creases of
time
lining your face
like some picture in a frame

I See You

If I get close
I can smell the

sweet taste of
wine between your lips

To ease the pain
of too much
Too much regret
laced with too much hurt
Too much
Too little
Too late

Morning Coffee

Morning Coffee
and scratchy kisses
Glances and little touches
Deep kisses
Dirty Dishes
and frameless pictures
Dresses that don't fit
and kids who are always having one
Bills and pills
Papers and thrills
Empty tanks
Empty hearts
Careless words
Once deep love
Memories of
Deep kisses

I Write Because I Must

I write because
I must
I write because it
Is who I am
Sometimes the words
fill my very being
to overflow
I must empty myself on paper
I always feel so
          much lighter
for my words have
found their space
and I have found my voice

Grab a Star

You get a short time to make a difference
to start a fire
watch it burn

The light that shines
will dim with time
You've got to grab a star
and ride it

Straight away

Free Cups and Sullen Looks

Free cups and sullen looks

Days end and days begin

Only you can feel the rain on your face as
we walk around this place

Cut my hair or grow it long this is how I feel
Stay here or leave this place
Horns blowing in the night

A Piece of Metal

A piece of metal
pierces her skin
The bullet cut through the day
with it came no reason
no name
no introduction
It came for twenty dollars
It came for a hundred
It took a father
It took a son
It pierced a heart
It broke a heart
It changed the world
It changed my world

Old Woman

I thought she said "old lemons"
And I kinda laughed
But what she really said was old woman

Well it's kinda the same isn't it I thought

And you know they never stop wearing heels
until they fall so many times they just give up

And they wheel themselves into Beauty Shops
And paint their nails in hospital beds

"Old Women" not "Old Lemons"

And she smiled and said it was an honor
and a blessing
to be an old woman

Hours for Dollars

Trading hours for dollars
for time is all we have

In the end

when the hours have faded
and the dollars have been spent

Is this all we were
Pawns in a game
Trading hours for dollars

Miss Annie

Her face a deep deep brown
From years of being
in the sun

She moved with the precision of time
I often see that scene in my head
Us riding up to visit her in our car
Cause in the South
the sound of a car
on gravel
is the only doorbell

I Saw Colors

When I was ten I
saw colors
Fridays were brown
Saturdays were Orange
And Sundays Red

Then when
I was sixteen
the colors faded
to the color of my first love's hair
Brown like pecan shells

Poem for Mr. Bell

There will be no rose petals for Mr. Bell
No ice cream
No cake
Today we will not pick
rice from his bride's hair

Or gather flowers in the wind

No dancing
No toast

The gown remains on the hanger
The cake was never eaten
The garter never tossed
They lost
in the dark
along with the dreams

We pick our battles
And sometimes
When you are
Black in America
Your battles pick you

Dedicated to the memory of Sean Bell who was shot by the police in New York City, in the borough of Queens, on November 25, 2006, following his bachelor party.

Again

Twenty were killed and a
world said, no not again
One was killed and again we said
How many more must die

Tears shadowed out the laughter
Another bullet
hit the ground

As life bled out today
Again

"You can kill the revolutionary, but you can't kill the revolution."
– Fred Hampton, Chairman and Member of the Illinois Black Panther Party,
assassinated by FBI in the predawn hours
of December 4, 1969, as he slept in bed.

Passing Through

People pass through
our lives
We remember them
the way they were
when they were with us

Like we capture them
in some time capsule
where they stay and never change

Time moves on
We move on
In our minds
In our hearts
they remain the same

A glass shatters and
we discover

They have moved on
just like us

Another Black Man

On the news today
so routine
What a shame
Another life
lost in the game

We shake our heads
Read the story
See his mother cry
Hear his father plead
to this prince of peace

Power
eludes these boys these men
Giants
Gods
Dads they will never become

And what of us
left behind
to wonder why
to close the wounds

Broken hearts
and empty shoes

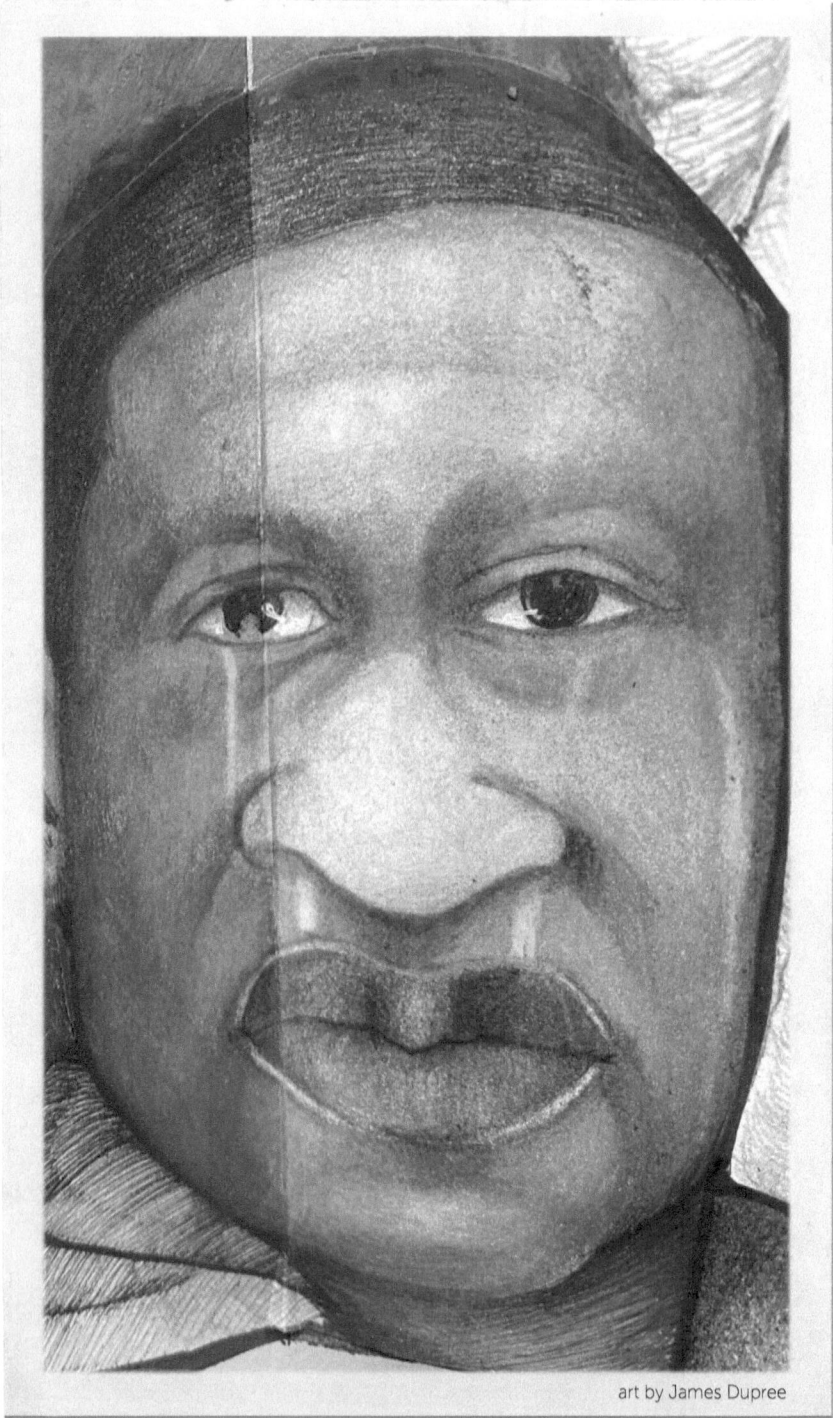

art by James Dupree

Memorial Day

He was killed on Memorial Day
The glass swept up
The boards taken down
Life will go on like it always does
The protest signs will become conversation
The news will move on
I guess until the next time
Will we forget
or will we change
His name now added to the list
of shame
Shame on America

But, the world took notice this time

Let us not let there be a next time

*Dedicated to the memory of George Floyd,
killed at the hands of the police.*
Memorial Day, 2020

The Ones

The ones we lost along the way
The ones with nothing left to lose
The scared ones
The I don't give a... ones

The ones we left behind
The ones who have no God
The ones who see no hope
The ones the teachers
cannot teach
The ones parents cannot parent
The ones police cannot police

I ask each one of us
What will become of the ones we leave behind?

Sister of Honey, Caramel, and Ebony

So many have written about your beauty
The colors of you
Honey to caramel to ebony and back
You are more than beauty
You are our pride
You rode the slave ships
You charted a course for our people
They beat you

Tied you up on that ship

You heard the ocean and closed your eyes
Imagined you were in a different place

You traveled back
Always wanting to go back
to what you knew

Here
They sold you
They defiled you
They took your babies from you

But I know
the heartbreak in your face

You fight
You march
You cry
You live
You die

You will never go back because
You are America
my beautiful sister of honey, caramel, and ebony

I Saw Her

I saw her
shopping bags in both hands
A look of tired digging
every line deeper into her face

I saw her
with a child in her arms
and a man far behind

I saw her
insulted
tears in her eyes
her spirit not broken… moving on

I saw her
beaten, pushed, pulled, raped by time and place
I saw her standing at the door of death
that was not supposed to be
Asking… Why me?
I saw her standing at a window wanting more, needing more

Believing she deserved more
And Yes… I have seen her a thousand times

Half

Almost here
and halfway there

And maybe yes
and sometimes no

Sometimes good
and sometimes bad

Making it all the way
and sometimes not

Sometimes running out
and sometimes running in

Enough

We always want more
Do more, Give more
Say more, Mean more

We feel as if we are never enough
But we have always been enough
Enough for our freedom

Enough for breath
Enough for ourselves

We have always been enough

The Queen

Do you see who I am
When you look at me
You glance at me like I'm not here
Did you not know
I once was a queen
I dined with Kings

I rode railroads that had no tracks
I built great cities

I had diamonds in my hair
and rubies on my toes

You ask me
How come I walk so proud

Well you see
The spirit of that Queen
Is me

She II

She lives in a place where only she can go

When she was young
it all lay before her

But now all her days are filled with pills
Regrets

Old movies and cigarettes

She seldom smiles in this
one-room-world of hers

Fleeting days and lonely nights
Streetlights shine through shades drawn tight

BREONNA

They call your name

Such a beautiful name too

They paint your name across the sky

Such a beautiful smile too

You look a lot like one of my cousins

I could have been you

But I AM YOU

I am Breonna too

Dedicated to the memory of Breonna Taylor, killed at the hands of the police.
March 13, 2020

Scarlet Weaver

A tapestry
he weaves together

The pieces of our lives
sometimes in fragments
scattered here and there, but

his artistry
reaches beyond
our eyes

He sees the finished cloth
scarlet

A beautiful
Complete
Life

I Am

the sun
the rain
the beginning
the end
the laughter
the silence

I am all there is
I can be the question
I can be the answer

For what am I?

I am the life you live

Your walking
Your living
Your dying
No beginning
And no end

See Me

You look ahead
And what do you see
Do you see me
Or do you see

The Black Man you think I am
The Black Man
The Angry Man

No that is not me
I am the friend
I am the father

Take that look of hate out of your eye
And see me
See me for who I am
See me for the man I am
See me as the friend
See me as the father
See me as the husband

See me as a man

Greyhound Bus to Jersey, 1977

He grabbed my hand
So much in love
This time
Our time
How could we know?

Hate would meet us
on that Greyhound bus

A perfect day becomes
the perfect hurt
A day gone awry

We are the wrong color
He one
I another
In the wrong time
on the wrong bus
riding with the worst kind of hate

The Look

Between their world and my world
that is where I live
I guess I have never gotten used to
the look

What are you doing here?
They asked

The little girl who didn't understand
Now the woman who does
will never get used to the look

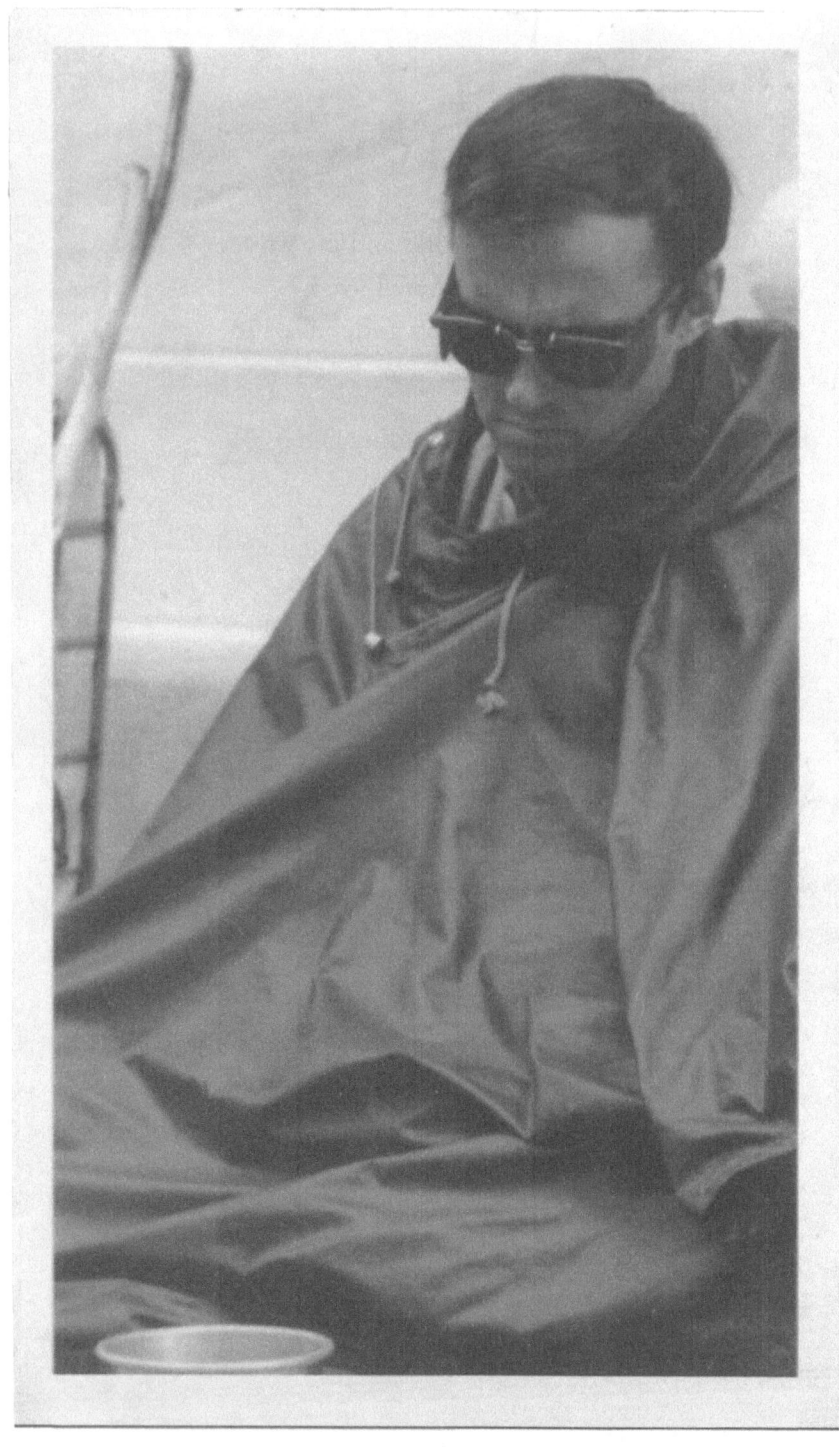

Lives

The lives we toss away
like empty soda bottles in summer
Broken lives
We all see them
lining our path
Putting cracks in the pictures of our perfect days
They cry out for dollars
For coins
We wonder
For Drinks?
For Drugs?
For cigarettes?

It must be hard
To beg
To cry
To not have
To want
To ask
To endure

Why do we wonder?
Do we not beg?

The Late

To find out you were gone
with the words "the late" next to your name
The years passed so quickly
And I so wanted you to be well
to be fine
to be somewhere…happy
to be smiling
to be in love
for someone to be holding you tight
Why did I never reach back for you?
Reach back for the smiles and the love
I left behind

Walls

Sometimes I want to just be...
where there are no
Walls

And the sky is
my ceiling

And the ground is the only floor I feel

And I see my reflection
in the eyes of
people who look like me

And the only music I hear is laughter
the laughter of my people

Words Will Make Us Think

Words will make us think, make us feel
and make us more, of who we are.
Words can change a nation, a person, the world
May the words in this poetry collage encourage
you to be more, do more
be you

Acknowledgments

I would like to sincerely give thanks to my African Ancestors who survived so I could dream.

I would like to thank all the strong Black men and women who fought the good fight and have inspired me to tell our story through poetry. I would also like to thank the pioneers in the struggle for our civil rights: men and women like John Lewis, Malcolm X, and Shirley Chisholm, the groundbreakers, the dreamers, the warriors, and the countless many who gave their lives.

My deep gratitude to all the great poets who inspired me to reach deep and write from my heart.

I sincerely thank all my friends and family who supported me through the journey of this book.

With love to my children, Jasmine and Phillip, for inspiring me to keep writing no matter what; and much thanks to my husband, Bill, who has been my constant friend, supporter, and encourager, despite the endless paper jams and endless copies.

Thank you to all the artists behind the poet, my beautiful niece Lauren Cruz for her artistic layout skills; designer Tim Ogline, who transformed my vision into a beautiful cover and interior. Also, thank you to artist James Dupree for his amazing portrait of George Floyd.

Thank you to all the photographers—and a special thanks to photographer William Lundy—who so graciously allowed me to use their photographs.

Special gratitude to my editor and publisher, Joy Stocke, who throughout this journey became my light and my friend.

To my God, who has allowed me to keep putting one foot in front of the other every day of this journey. Thank you.

About the Author

Zenobia Lundy, a daughter of the Great Migration, grew up and has lived most of her life in West Philadelphia. Her mother, Mary Michael, an inspiration for many of her poems, was born in South Carolina and came North where she became a day worker and later a nurse for her remaining years.

A graduate of the Philadelphia High School for Girls, with two years of undergraduate work at Temple University, Zenobia studied photography, which remains a passion, at the Antonelli School of Photography. Zenobia considers herself an urban gardener inspired by the cycle of life in nature.

In her late teens, Zenobia began writing poems—many of them autobiographical—and she has never stopped. For more than a decade she worked in public housing, managing Raymond Rosen Manor and Richard Allen Homes. Many of her poems are inspired by the people she served there. She currently works for the federal government.

Zenobia believes that poetry will always reflect the times we live in. "As a matter of fact, I wrote a verse today and it's etched in my mind," she says. "I saw a little girl going to school swinging her arms and smiling, and every one of her steps was filled confidence and grace. I imagined that little girl to be full of dreams. At the same time, I saw an old man sitting on the corner and wondered if his life was full of contentment or regrets, or both. But it's all part of the life cycle and our lives are pure poetry, if we choose to see it that way."

Zenobia currently lives in Philadelphia with her husband, William, and is working on her second book of poetry.

www.ingramcontent.com/pod-product-compliance
Lightning Source LLC
Chambersburg PA
CBHW020547080526
44583CB00013B/1028